Sweet Isidore John, Joseph

on the — you

Ba

May — you
throughout the year
and always

Joyful Colours of the Year

love + prayers
Godfather Peter, Maria,
Lani, Rupert, Hugo and
baby girl x

Joyful Colours of the Year

written by
Madeleine Hope Carroll

illustrated by
Lydia Grace Kadar-Kallen

Quis Ut Deus Press

Text copyright © 2017 by Madeleine Hope Carroll ISBN: 978-0-9984310-1-7

Illustrations copyright © 2017 by Lydia Grace Kadar-Kallen

Quis Ut Deus Press Logo copyright © 2013 by Mary Rose Kadar-Kallen

www.quisutdeuspress.com

All rights reserved. No portion of this book may be reproduced without express permission from the author and illustrator. A.M.D.G.

*For Mummy
who inspired my love of Nature in the first place.*

~ M.H.C.

For all my readers young and old who love the natural world.

~ L.G.K.

Glowing sunrise, spring dew,
Buds opening in clear hues.

Golden buttercups bursting forth,
Lively breezes from the north.

Fragrant heat, thundery showers,
Summer glory in rows of flowers.

Tall lime trees reach the sky,
Swifts and swallows weave and fly.

Waves breaking over pebble sands,
Heat hazes lifting over parched lands.

Mists linger on sills and ledges,
Blackberries ripen
 through hawthorn hedges.

Majestic oak trees,
acorns galore,
Squirrels scampering
on the forest floor.

Full moon, silver cloud,
Crashing sea, blue and loud.

Slate grey skies on a winter's morn,
As fallow deer run
 to greet the dawn.

Frost glistening on every blade,
Frozen pond in a frozen glade.

About the Author

Madeleine Carroll is a home-schooling mother of four lively children, and is expecting her fifth next spring. She lives in the countryside of Surrey in England. One of her favourite hobbies is taking long walks in the local Common where she can often catch glimpses of various types of wild-life, including deer, ducks, swans, geese and cuckoos, as well as free-ranging Dexter cattle. This is the first book that she has written about her beautiful native England.

About the Illustrator

Lydia Grace is a watercolour artist and illustrator who resides in Pennsylvania. When she isn't painting she plays the harp, bakes bread, reads books, watches birds, participates in living history events, and volunteers at church. She can most often be found with a cup of tea in her hand, sketchbook in tow, and trusty dog Jane at her side. This is her fourth picture book.

Printed in Great Britain
by Amazon